A small selection of children's cars from the Pennell family collection.

CHILDREN'S CARS

Paul Pennell

Shire Publications Ltd

CONTENTS

Set in 9 point Times roman and printed in Great Britain by C. I. Thomas & Sons (Haverfordwest) Ltd, Press Buildings, Merlins Bridge, Haverfordwest, Dyfed.

British Library Cataloguing in Publication Data available.

Editorial Consultant: Michael E. Ware, Curator of the National Motor Museum, Beaulieu.

ACKNOWLEDGEMENTS
   The author acknowledges with gratitude the assistance of the following in the preparation of this book: Aston Martin Lagonda Limited; Mike Cavanagh of the Cotswolds Motor Museum; Nigel Dawes; Richard Lines; Peter Brockes and Michael Ware of the National Motor Museum at Beaulieu; the Norsk Teknisk Museum, Norway. The photographs on pages 9, 25 and 32 are from the Photographic Library, National Motor Museum, Beaulieu. All the rest are from the author's collection.

COVER: *This superb late 1920s Peerless pedal car made by the Toledo Metal Wheel Company in the United States of America still delights children.*

BELOW: *The author in December 1960, eighteen months old and already showing a keen interest in cars, having just attached his first pedal car to his father's breakdown lorry.*

A very early French pedal car, dating from 1900-3, with centrally pivoting steering and 22 inch (55 cm) diameter rear wheels. The seating position in relation to the pedals betrays the car's bicycle ancestry. The child's pedal action would be almost the same as if riding a bicycle.

THE EARLY YEARS

As early motor cars became more familiar sights and interest in motoring grew it was natural that some children yearned for cars of their own rather than for more traditional toys such as rocking horses. The first children's pedal cars appeared very early in the twentieth century and, like the full-size motor cars which inspired them, were available only to the very rich. They were usually individually made to the owner's exact specification. The earliest pedal cars were of very simple design and construction and were based on early bicycle principles. Consequently, almost all British and European pedal cars made during this period employed a very simple chain-drive system. The pedals were mated to a sprocket drive wheel and were suspended centrally from the frame of the car. The solid rear axle was also fitted with a centrally positioned sprocket wheel and the drive was transmitted from the pedals through a bicycle-type chain.

A striking feature of most pedal cars of this period, shared with some of the earliest full-size cars, was that wheels of identical design but of different size were fitted to the front and rear of the car. The rear wheels were usually very large, some being as much as 24 inches (60 cm) in diameter, and the front wheels were

This wooden-bodied pedal car from the Cotswolds Motor Museum collection dates from around 1906 and is a good example of a car with full wings with steps and better than normal rear springing.

considerably smaller, which gave a distinctive stepped appearance to the pedal car. Both pairs of wheels had metal spokes.

The front axle was suspended centrally from the frame of the car and was normally centrally pivoting, which means that when the steering was turned on a lock the whole axle turned with the wheels, unlike the later form of steering which had a rigidly fixed front axle and just stub axles that pivoted and turned with the wheels.

The bodies were usually very simple and basic in design and normally had deeply cut-away side panels which eliminated the need for a door. Most were constructed entirely in wood but some better examples had properly coachbuilt bodies with a wooden framework which was then panelled with metal.

By about 1909-10 the pedal car had become established and was being made commercially in large numbers. Toy manufacturers were producing detailed

catalogues offering an already wide range of cars and accessories. G. and J. Lines of London, the leading British manufacturers of this period and toy makers since the late 1870s, sensibly tried to cater for as wide a range of buyers as possible and prices ranged from £2 for a very basic pedal car without a lamp or horn to as much as £18 10s for their most expensive model, the 'Featherweight Champion', which was fitted with all the available extras including Dunlop inflatable tyres, which gave a previously unobtainable quality of ride. This excellent model was very well constructed and finished and, more significantly, it incorporated some of the first real design improvements seen in commercially made pedal cars. Features such as the fully operative handbrake, the rigidly fixed front axle fitted with proper stub axles giving parallel wheel steering and the use of ball bearings throughout the design improved the engineering and made the car easier to use. Also worthy of note, although less

ABOVE: *A 1909-10 Gordon Bennett pedal car made by G. and J. Lines Limited of London. At this time they catalogued ten different models. The Gordon Bennett was in the medium price range and in this form cost £4.*

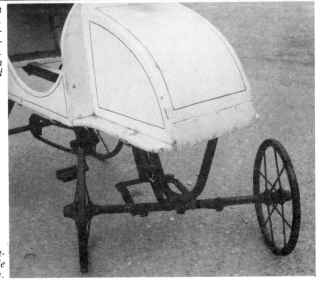

RIGHT: *With centrally pivoting steering the whole axle moves in relation to the body.*

significant, was the use for the first time of equal-size wheels. Although most of these features were available only on the most expensive model of the G. and J. Lines range, they clearly showed the scope for future developments.

As the market for pedal cars grew, the leading toy manufacturers were able to start introducing mass-production techniques to cater for the increased demand and very often found that they could not only dramatically increase production but also reduce their prices substantially and thus increase their sales still further.

In England this was clearly demonstrated by G. and J. Lines and in 1915-16 their most expensive pedal car was about £3 cheaper than the comparable car had been in 1909-10. Very little had changed in design during this time, the most obvious difference being that the body was now flush-sided and fitted with a single opening door, reflecting the trend in full-size car-body design. Minor additional features had been added, such as a dummy clock and speedometer, but it was essentially the original model.

The cheaper models also remained practically unchanged except for the universal use of equal-size wheels and the parallel wheel steering system, which had originally been available only on the dearest models.

In 1919 Lines Brothers Limited was founded by three sons of Joseph Lines, Walter, William and Arthur, who became the second generation of the family to enter the toy manufacturing business. Lines Brothers Limited, with their later trademark of Tri-ang, became one of the most famous names in toy manufacture and almost monopolised the British market in pedal cars over the next fifty years. Children's pedal cars, however, were never more than a small part of the overall business.

An early American pressed steel pedal car made by Gendron from around 1910. Unlike their European counterparts many American manufacturers were already using crank-type drive and mass-production techniques.

A British chain-drive two-seater pedal car of about 1915. This was a unique model, made to special order, and would have been expensive with its properly coachbuilt body.

The development of the pedal car has always been directly linked with that of the motor car reflecting, very gradually, improvements and changes in design. It is possible only to generalise as to the dates when changes were made. Very often manufacturers would decide to retain a popular design or feature despite the more general trend in their own range or amongst other manufacturers towards improvements and more modern and realistic designs. It was not uncommon to find some manufacturers producing the same pedal car model for ten years or more. This often makes precise dating impossible but it is usually possible to ascertain the years when a particular model was marketed, thus giving an approximate date of production.

This policy of retaining designs for long periods made very good business sense as there was no justification for spending time and money developing a new design to replace a popular model which sold well. This slow development was a trend that was to continue and it was not until the mid 1920s that completely new designs appeared.

ABOVE: *An early 1920s wooden-bodied chain-drive pedal car with steel wings and deep-buttoned seat. This was a popular design and was marketed by many motor factors under their own individual brand names. A de luxe version with windscreen and proper hood was also available.*

BELOW: *This late 1920s pressed steel Peerless pedal car made by the Toledo Metal Wheel Company is a superb example of an expensive American pedal car. It is amazingly well sprung and has very deeply pressed steel wings and drum-type headlamps so typical of the period. A novel feature is the folding case rack mounted on the running board.*

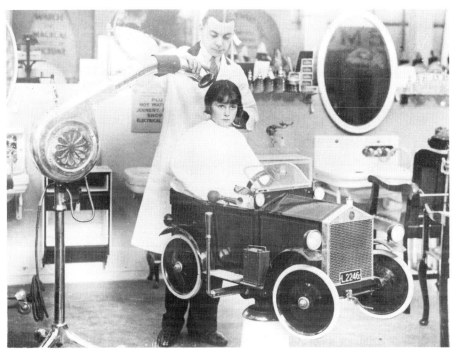

A mid 1920s pedal car bearing the thistle trademark used by G. and J. Lines of London and with a Rolls-Royce style radiator. Pedal cars were often adapted for use in barbers' shops during the 1920s, in Great Britain and the United States, to keep children happy while their hair was being cut and some barbers in Sweden still have pedal cars in their shops.

THE 1920s AND 1930s

Since the pedal car was first produced commercially, toy manufacturers had called many of their models after well known full-size motor cars. This was an attempt to influence potential buyers, fathers and sons alike, although the pedal cars often bore little or no resemblence to their full-size counterparts. The motor manufacturers felt that it did them no harm and that they gained some publicity from it.

In the United States of America, during the early 1920s, the American National Company of Toledo, Ohio, claimed to be the largest manufacturer of children's cars in the world. There were nearly forty different models in their catalogue, covering a wide price range, and numerous pages of optional accessories. Many cars had radiators accurately copied from famous full-size models, so a child could own a Cadillac, a Peerless or a Packard just like his father. This trend was excellent for sales and in Britain, Lines Brothers' 1924-5 catalogue illustrated pedal cars made with Rolls-Royce style radiators.

As parents and children were becoming more discriminating, the demand grew for toys which were better detailed and more realistic. This quest for realism was to lead to one of the most interesting of the Lines Brothers' pedal cars, produced during the late 1920s. It was a very well made, 6 foot long (180 cm) scale model of Sir Henry Segrave's famous record-breaking Sunbeam and was available in several forms. It was a most unusual pedal car and the body could be finished in polished aluminium or painted in British racing green. Lines Brothers' advertisements claimed that Segrave himself had supervised its construction. Priced at £12 14s it was one of their most expensive models.

During this period their range also included a wide variety of pedal cars bearing reasonably accurate copies of motor manufacturers' radiators. The Bullnose Morris was one of their most popular models but the range also included Rolls-Royce, Vauxhall, Buick, Chevrolet, Daimler and many other popular marques. The cars, however, were only loosely based on their full-size counterparts, unlike the racing Sunbeam pedal car, which was made as an accurate scale model.

In France Eureka was producing a very wide range of crank drive, pressed steel pedal cars made to resemble the most popular French marques such as Bugatti, Citroen and Renault. Other large-volume European manufacturers such as the long-established Italian toy firm, Giordani, were producing similar ranges by the same techniques.

Lines Brothers, however, chose to persist with traditional coachbuilt construction for a large part of their production, particularly for the most expensive models, although a significant change was the transition from chain drive to crank drive. By 1930 most of their production was concentrated on crank-drive models although some chain-drive pedal cars were still made.

In March 1931 Lines Brothers Limited

A very original 1920s Lines Brothers Limited pedal car. The LB 2376 registration on the number plate is interesting as the telephone number for the company works at 761 Old Kent Road, London SE15, was New Cross 2376. The other commonly used registration number was LB 3067, which was the telephone number of the main works at Morden Road, Merton, London SW19.

ABOVE: *This Lines Brothers Limited Tri-ang pedal car with Bullnose Morris style radiator and striking polished aluminium body was catalogued in 1930 as a Brooklands racing car model and cost three guineas. A dearer version fitted with Dunlop inflatable tyres was also available and cost five guineas.*

BELOW: *An interesting comparison showing the enormous change in design between 1900 and 1935 and clearly showing how, by using crank-type drive, lower body lines could be achieved.*

A display of pedal cars at the Cotswolds Motor Museum, predominantly featuring Tri-ang examples from Lines Brothers Limited. These range from the late 1920s Buick (centre), with petrol can and toolbox mounted on the running board, to the Daimler sports car (top left), which was introduced in the late 1930s and was still catalogued by Tri-ang in 1951.

registered 'Tri-ang' as a trademark and later that year the name of the company works was changed from Triangtois Works to Tri-ang Works. Early in 1932 Lines Brothers took over G. and J. Lines, Joseph Lines having died on 31st December 1931, and the famous thistle trademark disappeared.

Dates such as these are often a useful guide in dating some of their pedal cars, as those models fitted with instrument panels have the name of the works printed on them.

The top-of-the-range Vauxhall model introduced by Lines in 1932 was one of the most attractive and best proportioned designs they ever made and achieved the rare distinction of looking more like a proper car than a toy. Today it is highly sought after and considered by many collectors to be the ultimate Lines Brothers pedal car. The Vauxhall had a

ABOVE: *The top-of-the-range Lines Brothers Limited Tri-ang Vauxhall with its beautifully styled body was a superb pedal car and is much sought after today.*

BELOW: *A very sporting Lines Brothers Limited Tri-ang Greyhound pedal car with wooden body and MG-style radiator. It was an expensive model, costing six guineas in 1935, and was fitted with chrome wire wheels and inflatable tyres.*

ABOVE: *An outstanding Lines Brothers Limited Tri-ang Buick of the mid 1930s. This was the most expensive model and had a high-quality tubular chassis upon which was fitted a properly coachbuilt body with single opening door and dickey seat.*

LEFT: *The elegantly shaped back of the Buick with the dickey seat in the closed position. Note also the beautifully shaped rear quarter bumpers made to match the front bumper.*

A late 1930s pressed steel pedal car in original condition on display at the Cotswolds Motor Museum. It is a good example of the trend amongst toy manufacturers of imitating the streamlined airflow car designs of the period.

coachbuilt wooden body with a single opening door and an opening boot for carrying toys or small items of luggage. The bonnet and boot lid were made of aluminium and the wings were made of steel. The car was crank-driven, had wheels fitted with Dunlop 12½ by 2¼ inch (32 by 6 cm) inflatable tyres and had excellent leaf-spring suspension with proper spring shackles. It had a toolbox mounted on the running board and miniature petrol and oil cans. The car cost £5 12s but a cheaper version without inflatable tyres was also available at £3 17s.

At the other end of the range the cheapest Lines Brothers Vauxhall, with a very basic pressed steel body, cost a little over £1. It was also possible to buy separately all the necessary components

for chain-drive pedal cars, such as wheels, steering gear and pedal gear, from toy shops or motor factors. This enabled a father who had some practical ability and time to spare to build a pedal car to his own specification and more cheaply. Unfortunately many home-made pedal cars were poorly constructed and finished and today most serious collectors are not interested in them unless they are exceptionally good.

During the late 1930s small pressed steel pedal cars dominated the market, giving ever increasing sales. Many reflected the popular streamlined airflow designs of the time. Some excellent pedal cars were still made but the years of the finest children's cars had passed.

ABOVE AND BELOW: *The famous Pomeroy Vauxhall with its superbly made miniature Vauxhall Prince Henry radiator is still in beautiful condition and now part of the Nigel Dawes collection.*

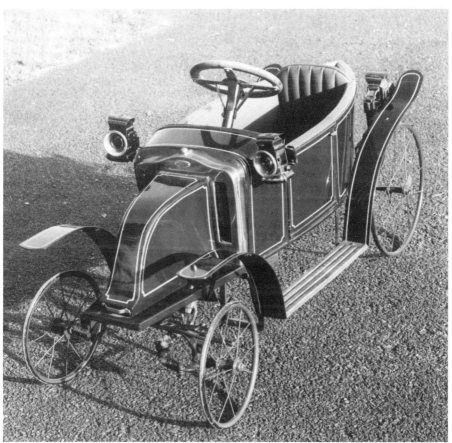

A unique Renault pedal car of about 1913 made by J. Farizon of France. It is an exquisite pedal car with a beautifully shaped metal-panelled coachbuilt body, elaborate rear springs, brass radiator and very unusual double chain-drive pedal system.

LUXURY AND SPLENDOUR

In the early days motoring was extremely expensive and limited to the wealthy. It was quite normal at this time, when buying a quality car, to purchase the car in chassis form. The owner would commission a coachbuilder to design and build a body which was then trimmed and equipped to the exact needs and specifications of the buyer. This practice was extended to some pedal cars and the coachbuilder would produce a unique car which was often a miniature based on the full-size family car.

There was also a growing awareness of the advertising potential of children's cars and businessmen and motor manufacturers were soon exploiting this new field. One of the first such ventures was undertaken in the United States by the Reo Motor Company in 1906, when they produced a small number of superb miniatures of their current two-cylinder car. These models were powered by compressed air and were exhibited at various motor shows.

In 1912 F. S. Bennet, the Cadillac

concessionaire in England, commissioned the London coachbuilders J. Lockwood and Company of Islington to produce a perfect miniature Cadillac built to a scale of two-fifths full size. It was to be powered solely by the newly introduced Cadillac electric self-starter so that the model would not only be a major attraction in its own right but would also, more importantly, demonstrate the efficiency and effectiveness of the Cadillac combined starting, lighting and ignition system.

The finished model was outstanding and was shown at the Paris Motor Show of 1912. It attracted an enormous amount of attention and was bought soon afterwards by Queen Alexandra as a present for her nephew, Crown Prince Olav of Norway. Before the car was delivered its top speed was reduced from 16 to 7 mph (26 to 11 km/h), as a precaution, and Bennet showed the nine-year-old Crown Prince how to drive it. The model Cadillac was well looked after by Prince Olav

and in November 1948 he presented it to the Norsk Teknisk Museum, Oslo, where it is still carefully preserved. An identical Cadillac model was later made for King Rama I of Thailand and given to his son Prince Chula. It was subsequently brought to England and has fortunately remained in the possession of the Chakrabongse family. Still in beautiful original condition, it can be seen at the London Toy and Model Museum.

In 1915 a very attractive child's Vauxhall 'Prince Henry' was made for Laurence Pomeroy junior, son of the famous engineer who designed the original car, which many believe to have been the first true British sports car. It was made in the Vauxhall Motors workshop and was restored there nearly forty years later, in 1953. It is now owned by the motoring enthusiast and collector Nigel Dawes.

In the 1920s several outstanding children's cars were made. In 1924, Leslie Wilson, a Birmingham engineer, started production of a very fine Alvis pedal car

The outstanding electrically powered 1912 Cadillac preserved in the Norsk Teknisk Museum and built by J. Lockwood and Company of Islington, London, appears perfect in every detail and is undoubtedly one of the world's finest children's cars.

The electrically powered Type 52 Bugatti of 1927 is an exquisitely made child's car, almost indistinguishable from its full-size counterpart in photographs, and it is one of the world's most sought-after children's cars.

which was a perfectly scaled-down model of the Alvis racing car that had won the previous year's 200 mile (320 km) race at Brooklands. This was not a financial success and only about fifty examples were made. During 1925, J. F. Stevenson, owner of the Belfast garage Victor Robb and Company, made a child's car which could be used to demonstrate the ease of operation of his patented jacking system, introduced two years earlier. As the garage held a Clyno agency, the child's car was made as a perfectly scaled-down Clyno fitted with its own miniature jacking system, in this way promoting both products. The Clyno was exhibited at the New York Motor Show in January 1926 and at the London Motor Show in October of that year.

Citroen of France had been making small toy Citroen cars for two years when, in 1925, they started to produce an extremely attractive pedal car. It was

based on the 5CV Cloverleaf model and was one-third full size. The body was of steel construction and the wings, unusually for this period, were made of wood. There was careful thought behind the Citroen toy business. André Citroen believed that if children were proud of their Citroen toys it could start an association with his company which would last until they grew up and bought motor cars.

The successful 5CV pedal car was followed in 1928 by the introduction of an even finer child's car, the Citroenette, which was electrically powered and based on the full-size C6 car. It was a superb model, well equipped and well finished, with a steel body and wings. The electric motor had a built-in differential and gave a top speed of 6 mph (10 km/h).

At the 1927 Milan Motor Show the remarkable electrically powered child's Bugatti, the Type 52, was launched, based on the successful Type 35 Grand

19

This superb 1931 French Eureka Bugatti tandem pedal car has two sets of pedals so both driver and passenger can pedal together. It captures the spirit of the grand touring cars of the early 1930s that graced the French boulevards.

Prix car and made to the same superior standards as the full-size Bugatti car. It had a superb forged, circular-section, nickel-plated front axle with half-elliptic springs going through it. The wheels were cast aluminium with integral brake drums and the cable-operated brakes worked on all four wheels. The 12 volt electric motor drove the right-hand rear wheel and gave a top speed of 10 mph (16 km/h). A Type 52 was displayed at the 1927 London Motor Show at Olympia and was priced at £60.

In addition to their normal wide range of children's cars toy manufacturers pro-duced some extremely fine and presti-gious top-of-the range models. Although these cannot be compared with some of the cars previously mentioned, they were exceptionally good considering that toy manufacturers had to be strictly governed by commercial viability and the need for large sales. Eureka in France produced some excellent pressed steel pedal cars, examples based on Bugattis of the late 1920s and early 1930s being particularly popular. Lines Brothers in England also produced some exceptional cars and in the main chose to retain traditional coachbuilt construction. Their most prestigious model was the electrically powered model based on the Rolls-Royce of the 1930s.

In the United States there were many manufacturers of children's cars, the largest of which was the American National Company of Toledo, Ohio, which produced some exceptional pedal cars during the 1920s. Among the finest were the rare and much sought-after Packard fixed-head coupé and the tandem two-seater Packard Phaeton, equipped with two sets of pedals.

Since the Second World War substantially fewer outstanding children's cars have been made. A notable exception was the James Bond Aston Martin produced for Prince Andrew and presented to Her Majesty the Queen when she visited the Aston Martin factory at Newport Pagnell, Buckinghamshire, on 4th April 1966. The project to build the miniature car, called the DB 007 special, involved a specialist team of over thirty people from the various factory departments. The car was electrically powered, took 2½ months to build and incorporated practically all the electrical gadgetry and special features associated with the full-size James Bond Aston Martin, made famous in the films *Goldfinger* and *Thunderball*. The specification was extremely complex and included electrically operated revolving front and rear number plates so that English, French or Swiss registrations could be selected. The front and rear bumpers were fitted with electrically operated extending overriders and

The electrically powered Lines Brothers Rolls-Royce introduced in 1933 was intended to be the ultimate in British children's cars and despite a price of 30 guineas sold well, with a number going to the families of Indian maharajas.

twin dummy machine-guns were concealed behind the front sidelamp lenses, which were opened and closed by a spring-loaded lever below the dashboard. When the lever was pushed forward the lenses opened to reveal the machine-guns, and when the lever was released they automatically closed again. An electrically operated bullet-proof shield was concealed in the boot and electrically operated water jets were hidden in the rear light reflectors.

A special ground radar system was fitted, with the display screen cleverly concealed behind the radio speaker grille on the dashboard. Concealed in the exhaust pipe was a smoke discharger which took replaceable cartridges and was activated by pressing a red button on the right-hand side of the dashboard. A Luger pistol with silencer and two transistorised two-way radio units completed the specification. An identical model was made and presented to Prince Reza, the son of the Shah of Persia.

The cost of building the two DB 007 specials cannot be accurately calculated. It was estimated that had the people who worked on the project not freely given their time and had various suppliers not donated parts each car would have cost as much as a full-size Aston Martin DB 6, which retailed at £4,998 in 1966.

A 1933 Lines Brothers Limited electric Rolls-Royce alongside a 1926 Rolls-Royce Twenty Tourer.

ABOVE: *The rolling chassis of the electrically powered Aston Martin DB 007 specially made for Prince Andrew shows the complexity of design and substantial tubular frame construction.*

BELOW: *Several of the car's James Bond features: the electrically operated revolving number plates and extending overriders on the bumper, and the sidelight lenses which open to reveal machine guns.*

ABOVE AND BELOW: *The Austin Pathfinder of 1949-50 was a beautiful racing pedal car which could accommodate a large child. Its robust construction and large production has ensured that comparatively large numbers have survived. Under the bonnet is a dummy twin-cam engine fitted with proper spark plugs.*

Three important royal cars photographed at Buckingham Palace before going on loan to the National Motor Museum at Beaulieu for a special 1983 Christmas exhibition. On the left is an American petrol-engined Midget Racer made for Prince Charles. In the centre is the Aston Martin DB 007 special made for Prince Andrew and on the right is an electric 1928 Citroen which was later updated and fitted with a Daimler radiator for Prince Charles.

FROM 1945 TO THE PRESENT

During the period of reorganisation and rebuilding following the Second World War manufacturers and suppliers began the transition from wartime work to producing normal consumer goods again. In Great Britain priority had to be given to exports and only a small percentage of production was available for the home market. Many raw materials, such as steel, were in short supply and it was against this background of austerity that toy manufacturers resumed production. Like most motor manufacturers, their early postwar products were simply con-

tinuations of their pre-war designs.

The first new pedal car of merit to be manufactured was made by the Austin Motor Company. In 1946 Sir Leonard Lord, the company chairman, had first conceived the idea of establishing a special factory in Wales, to be situated in an area of high unemployment, specifically to provide jobs for former coal miners forced to leave the industry as a result of the serious lung disease pneumoconiosis. The factory was to build children's Austin pedal cars and, as the primary function was to create employment, it was to be run on a non-profitmaking basis and most of the funding for the project was to come from the government. The steel for the production of the miniature body shells was to be provided from the small offcuts of scrap metal left over from production at the main Austin Longbridge plant. The official opening took place on 5th July 1949 and the 24,500 square foot (2275 square metre) factory employed fifty men.

The first pedal car produced was called the Pathfinder and was based in appearance on the famous pre-war Jamieson Austin 750 twin-cam racing car, which had created so much publicity for Austin between 1936 and 1939. The Pathfinder was a fine pedal car with an extremely strong pressed steel body. Twin buckle-up straps secured the bonnet, which, when removed, revealed a dummy twin-cam engine fitted with four proper spark plugs and leads. Other features included an adjustable handbrake which operated

an asbestos-lined drum brake, well detailed dummy instruments, an aeroscreen and a fish-tail exhaust. The seat was padded and trimmed in leathercloth and the back hinged forward to reveal a useful storage compartment. The pressed steel hubs ran on roller bearings and the pressed steel wheels were easily removed and were fitted with Dunlop 12½ by 2¼ inch (32 by 6 cm) inflatable tyres. The pedals could be easily adjusted for leg reach and a crank-drive pedal system was employed, with the drive taken through the right-hand rear wheel only, to give a differential action. The overall appearance and finish of the Pathfinder was excellent, but it was an expensive pedal car at £25 including purchase tax. A production figure of 250 a week was hoped for but never reached and after a year the Pathfinder was dropped and replaced by a new model. This was based in appearance on the Austin A40 Devon and called the Austin Junior Forty Roadster, which, not surprisingly, was

The Austin J40 introduced in 1950 was an outstanding pedal car that set the standards by which others were judged. Their long production run has ensured that they will never become rare but they will always be popular, particularly amongst new collectors. Many are still in regular use at fairgrounds and in road safety displays.

ABOVE AND RIGHT: *The back of the Austin J40 and a view of the well detailed dashboard. The horn push can be seen in the centre of the steering wheel.*

invariably abbreviated to J40.

The J40 was even better detailed and more realistic than its predecessor, and equally robust as it was designed and constructed in the same manner. Amongst its most popular features were the properly hinged bonnet and boot. The bonnet opened to reveal the dummy engine fitted with four proper spark plugs and the batteries which powered the working headlamps and horn. The J40 also had a miniature replica of the 'flying A' bonnet mascot carried by the full-size Austin models. The mascots were later deemed to be potentially dangerous and late J40 models, from 1968-9 onwards, were produced without a mascot and with a plain bonnet moulding. The J40,

ABOVE: *The 1964-9 Tri-ang pressed steel E-type Jaguar pedal car was a comparatively poor representation but was very popular. With the growth in interest in all Jaguars and particularly E-types these pedal cars are becoming much sought after by Jaguar enthusiasts.*

BELOW: *A well modelled French-made pressed steel Citroen DS21 Convertible pedal car dating from the late 1960s.*

The very realistic Meynell and Phillips Limited 4½ litre Le Mans Bentley. This example has been extensively modified by its owner, Nigel Dawes, to make it appear even more realistic.

although always expensive, proved to be very popular and had a long production run. It was manufactured until September 1971, by which time 32,098 had been produced, with a large percentage being exported.

During the 1950s and 1960s Tri-ang produced a very large range of children's cars, most of which were pedal-powered but including a few that were electrically powered.

In 1955-6 an electrically powered version of their popular 'Super Eight' racing car was catalogued and during 1957-8 an unusual electrically powered Mercedes-style racing car was available. In 1964 they introduced an attractive moulded plastic Rolls-Royce pedal car styled after the Rolls-Royce Silver Cloud 3 Convertible. A moulded plastic Triumph TR4 and a metal-bodied E-type Jaguar were other new additions to the range.

In 1968 Antique Automobiles Limited of Peterborough introduced a superb reproduction of the famous child's Type 52 Bugatti, available powered either by electricity (£400) or petrol (£450). In 1969, at H. R. Owen's London showroom, an electrically powered child's Bentley was launched, based on a supercharged 1929 4½ litre Le Mans car. The Bentley had a fibreglass body and was made by Meynell and Phillips Limited of Burton upon Trent. It cost £250 in quick assembly form.

During the 1970s and 1980s there has been a major revival in quality children's cars and a vast range is available. There are modern Rolls-Royces, Mercedes, Ferraris and Volkswagen Beetles and even replicas of racing cars such as the Maserati 250F, world-famous in the mid 1950s. The prices also vary widely from several hundred pounds to several thousand pounds.

Individuals and museums are increasingly interested in collecting children's cars. In England the first major

29

ABOVE: *This very pretty fibreglass-bodied Citroen 5CV pedal car manufactured by Lely Small Cars cost £680 in 1984.*

BELOW: *An exquisite electrically powered reproduction child's 250F Maserati made by Maserati specialist Richard Crump of Waltham Cross, Hertfordshire. It is constructed to the highest standards and has a beautiful hand-made aluminium body. The finned cast aluminium brake drums and the polished bronze front-suspension wishbones emphasise the quality and the great attention to detail. The price in 1984 was £3,000.*

exhibition was held at the National Motor Museum at Beaulieu, Hampshire, at Christmas 1983 and was a great success. In the United States of America the interest is far greater and there are now regular pedal car shows, at some of which cash prizes are offered for the best exhibits.

There are also a number of specialist companies reproducing previously unobtainable parts and undertaking expensive full restorations to the highest possible standards. Many children's cars which have been restored are of much better quality than the originals and are regarded more as art objects than toys.

BRITISH AND AMERICAN TERMS

The following is a list of some British automotive terms with their American equivalents.

British	American
bonnet	hood
boot	trunk
dashboard	instrument panel
dickey seat	rumble seat
hood	top
number plate	license plate
petrol	gasoline
windscreen	windshield
wing	fender

A realistic fibreglass-bodied electrically powered Austin Seven 'Chummy' made by Royle Cars Limited of Staindrop near Darlington. It is well detailed and comes complete with hood and sidescreens and cost £3,195 in 1985.

FURTHER READING

Very little has been written about children's cars and the following are the only publications which cover the subject adequately. They can usually be obtained from the specialist motoring bookshops.

Gardiner, Gordon, and Morris, Alistair. *The All Colour Directory of Metal Toys*. Salamander, 1984.
Massucci, Edoardo. *Bebe Auto*. Automobilia, 1982.
'The Mini-World of Francis Mortarini'. *Automobile Quarterly*, volume 6, number 4, spring 1968.
Van Rooten, Court. 'Putting the Kids on Wheels'. *Automobile Quarterly*, volume 12, number 1, spring 1974.

PLACES TO VISIT

There are no museums solely devoted to children's cars, but the following usually have examples on display. Intending visitors are advised to find out the times of opening before making a special visit and to check that items of interest are on display.

Cotswolds Motor Museum, The Old Mill, Bourton-on-the-Water, Cheltenham, Gloucestershire. Telephone: Bourton-on-the-Water (0451) 21255.
Lakeland Motor Museum, Holker Hall, Cark in Cartmel, Grange-over-Sands, Cumbria. Telephone: Flookburgh (044 853) 509.
London Toy and Model Museum, 23 Craven Hill, London W2 3EN. Telephone: 01-262 7905 or 9450.
National Motor Museum, John Montagu Building, Beaulieu, Brockenhurst, Hampshire SO4 7ZN. Telephone: Beaulieu (0590) 612345.
Toy Museum, 42 Bridge Street Row, Chester, Cheshire. Telephone: Chester (0244) 316251.

The Children's Motor Show held in the Hall of Fame at the National Motor Museum at Beaulieu during the 1983 Christmas period.

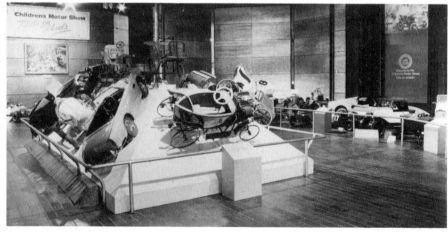